P9-DNZ-518

# Christmas in Switzerland

# Christmas in Switzerland

## Christmas Around the World
## From World Book

World Book, Inc.
a Scott Fetzer company

CHICAGO   LONDON   SYDNEY   TORONTO

# Staff

**Publisher Emeritus**
William H. Nault

**President**
John Frere

**Vice President,**
 **Editor in Chief**
Dick Dell

## Editorial

**Managing Editor**
Maureen Mostyn Liebenson

**Associate Editor**
Karen Zack Ingebretsen

**Writer**
Lisa Klobuchar

**Permissions Editor**
Janet T. Peterson

**Director of Research**
Mary Norton

**Researcher**
Lynn Durbin

## Art

**Executive Director**
Roberta Dimmer

**Art Director**
Wilma Stevens

**Senior Designer**
Brenda B. Tropinski

**Senior Photographs Editor**
Sandra Dyrlund

**Photographs Editor**
Kelly Mountain

## Product Production

**Vice President, Production and**
 **Technology**
Daniel N. Bach

**Director of Manufacturing/Pre-Press**
Sandra Van den Broucke

**Manufacturing Manager**
Barbara Podczerwinski

**Senior Production Manager**
Randi Park

**Manufacturing Production**
 **Assistant**
Trisha Ripp

**Proofreader**
Anne Dillon

## Direct Marketing

**Marketing Manager**
John Deneen

**Director, Product Development**
Paul Kobasa

World Book wishes to thank the following individuals for their contributions to *Christmas in Switzerland:* Sascha Brawer, Sarah Figlio, Dianne Kiefer-Dicks, Sara Schödler, Katie Sharp, and Brigitte Shidrawi.

World Book, Inc.
525 W. Monroe
Chicago, IL 60661

ISBN: 0-7166-0895-2
LC: 95-60193

Printed in the United States of America
1 2 3 4 5 6 7 8 9 10 99 98 97 96 95

# Contents

# A Many~Faceted Christmas

Switzerland, a small country tucked in the heart of central Europe, is a place where winter holiday traditions thrive. From wild, masked winter processions to intimate domestic Christmas Eve celebrations, the holiday season in Switzerland is a unique blend of old and new; Catholic and Protestant; and German, French, and Italian influences. Indeed, the traditions that surround this holy holiday demonstrate the true diversity of the people who call this very special country home.

Die Schweiz. Suisse. Svizzera. This trio of official names for Switzerland reflects not only the country's three official languages—German, French, and Italian—but also its multilingual, multicultural identity. In addition to these languages, a small percentage of Swiss people speak yet another—Romansh, which has been designated a national language. But the Swiss are diverse not only in language; their religious beliefs differ, as well. About half are Roman Catholic, while 45 percent are Protestant.

Despite their cultural differences, the people of the 26 cantons (political divisions) and half-cantons that comprise the nation of Switzerland take pride in their country. Today, Switzerland is notable chiefly for its long tradition of neutrality, as well as its almost legendary cleanliness and order and, of course, its high standard of living.

## Shared traditions

While Christmas in Switzerland is rich in tradition, it is safe to say that no single "typically Swiss" Christmas tradition exists. The people of each region celebrate the season in their own way. In fact, people in one region may be completely unaware of customs observed elsewhere. But while celebrations across the country have their unique hues, a closer look at the Swiss holiday customs and traditions reveals that many of them have been influenced over the years by neighboring countries.

By far the majority of the Swiss—about 70 percent—speak a form of German called *Schwyzerdütsch* (Swiss-German). Swiss-German-speaking citizens live in the country's northern, eastern, and central cantons. In the west, French is the dominant language, spoken by about 20 percent of the Swiss. Southern Switzerland is home to the nearly 10 percent of the population whose first language is Italian. Romansh-speakers, who make up less than 1 percent of the Swiss population, live in the mountain valleys of the canton of Graubünden in Switzerland's southeast. Romansh is a romance language that is a mixture of Latin, Italian, and German.

Although certain traditions, such as the Advent wreath, the Christmas tree, and St. Nicholas, are observed by most of the Swiss, each region tends to vary their emphasis. For example,

Pages 6-7:
While Switzerland is a land of diverse people, there's one thing on which they all can agree: There's no place like their homeland to enjoy the festivities of winter, whether it's sharing a sleigh ride, celebrating Christmas, or welcoming the New Year.

some regions, especially the north and central Swiss-German-speaking Catholic ones, celebrate the beginning of the Christmas season with a visit from St. Nicholas, or *Samichlaus*, as he is called in the Swiss-German dialect, on December 5 and 6. Dressed in a long red robe, carrying a staff, and accompanied by his frightening sidekick Schmutzli, St. Nicholas brings sweets, nuts, tangerines, and other small goodies to the children who have been good. Naughty children must beware, however. The mean-spirited Schmutzli totes a large sack in which to haul them off. In other areas, however, especially Protestant ones, St. Nicholas makes only incidental appearances.

Even from family to family, holiday traditions vary. Protestant households tend to celebrate Christmas with less fuss and

Christmas trees and snowmen are beloved symbols of the season throughout Switzerland. Here, families shop for trees on a snow day, while a young boy crowns his friend in an old woolen hat.

# Unity in Diversity

Switzerland is a country of many different people and cultures. Brought together in a pact to defend one another, the Swiss relish their diversity and take pride in their unity. The citizens who comprise the different regions of Switzerland have adopted and nurtured their ways of life from their German, French, and Italian ancestors. And they defend these ways of life in the same spirit of independence that has made Switzerland famous.

The country of Switzerland lies just east of France and is less than 1 percent as large as the contiguous states of the United States. Today about 6,955,000 people call this country home, although most family trees branch out to other countries. In fact, Switzerland has a higher percentage of foreign-born residents than any other European country. Most of the Swiss live on a plateau that extends across the middle of the country

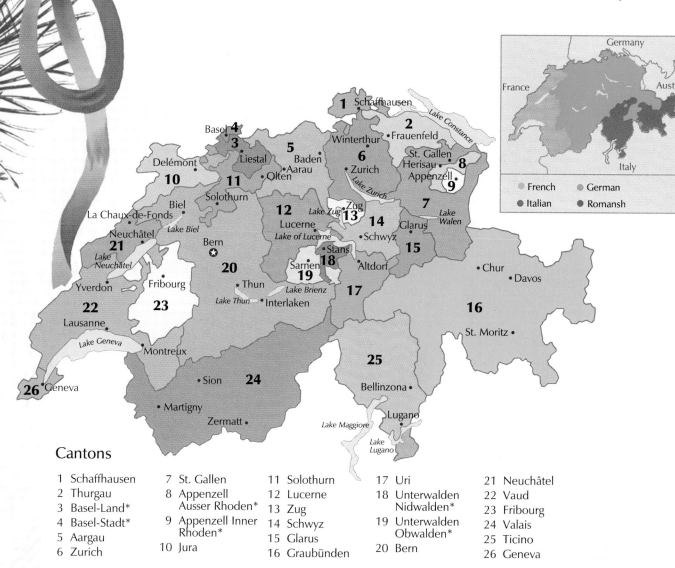

## Cantons

| | | | | |
|---|---|---|---|---|
| 1 Schaffhausen | 7 St. Gallen | 11 Solothurn | 17 Uri | 21 Neuchâtel |
| 2 Thurgau | 8 Appenzell Ausser Rhoden* | 12 Lucerne | 18 Unterwalden Nidwalden* | 22 Vaud |
| 3 Basel-Land* | 9 Appenzell Inner Rhoden* | 13 Zug | 19 Unterwalden Obwalden* | 23 Fribourg |
| 4 Basel-Stadt* | | 14 Schwyz | | 24 Valais |
| 5 Aargau | 10 Jura | 15 Glarus | 20 Bern | 25 Ticino |
| 6 Zurich | | 16 Graubünden | | 26 Geneva |

*Half cantons

Merry Christmas from Switzerland

between the the Swiss Alps and the Jura Mountains. Switzerland's richest farmland is in this region, as are most of the large cities and manufacturing industries. The Swiss Alps cover about 60 percent of Switzerland, but less than a fifth of the people live there. The most populated cities of Switzerland include Zurich, Basel, Geneva, Lausanne, and the country's capital, Bern.

The Swiss have a long history of defending their freedom. During the 1200's, the Habsburg family controlled much of Switzerland. Fearing the family's growing power, the free men of what are today the *cantons* (states) of Schwyz, Uri, and Unterwalden joined forces. In 1291 the three regions declared their freedom and vowed to help defend each other against foreign rulers. Their pledge was the beginning of the Swiss Confederation. The confederation came to be known as Switzerland, taking its name from the canton of Schwyz.

By the 1400's Switzerland became a strong military power and fought several wars in an effort to gain land. In 1515, however, the Swiss suffered a crushing defeat at the hands of the French. Switzerland soon adopted a policy of neutrality, which was later guaranteed at the Congress of Vienna (1814-1815).

In 1848, Switzerland adopted the Swiss Constitution, which was revised in 1874. The Constitution established a federal republic in which political powers are divided between the central government and the governments of the 23 cantons—3 of which are divided into half-cantons. The cantons' and half-cantons' independence is ensured by the Constitution. They are real states, each with its own constitution, legislatures, executives, and judiciaries. Legislative power rests with the Swiss people or with a parliament electd by them. So even the cantons, as with almost all aspects of Swiss culture, are united in diversity.

ceremony than do Catholic households. Moreover, in many families the parents come from different language regions, so the traditions have become even more blended. Add to this pattern the texture of the numerous ancient folk customs kept alive throughout the country—Switzerland perhaps leads all other modern Western nations in the number of folk traditions it has preserved—and a rich tapestry of holiday celebration emerges. It is this very variety that can be said to be typically Swiss.

Sacred church services unite the Swiss during the holy season of Christmas.

But for all the differences in language and custom, a number of Christmas traditions are quite similar throughout Switzerland. Some of these are the Advent wreath, the Christmas tree, Christmas carols, gift giving, a mouth-watering meal either on Christmas Eve or Christmas Day, and sacred church services. Swiss Radio also unites the people of Switzerland during the holy season with a popular series of sing-along caroling broadcasts that begins on the first Sunday of Advent. Radio stations mail song books in advance to more than 60,000 people in private homes, schools, children's homes, and senior citizens' centers so that listeners can sing along at home. Those who would rather gather together in song can join the audience at the studio to take part in the live broadcasts.

## Christianity arrives in Switzerland

The celebration of the birth of Christ on December 25 probably began in the Roman Empire around A.D. 326. One of Switzerland's most beloved patron saints, St. Gall, was responsible for bringing Christianity and the celebration of Christmas to Switzerland in the early A.D. 600's. And although the worship of Christ eventually replaced the old gods and goddesses, Switzerland is no different from the rest of northern Europe, in that many of its Christmas traditions are adaptations of pre-Christian customs. The pagan custom of decorating the home with greenery to symbolize fertility in the dead of winter, for example, survives in the form of the Christmas tree and the hanging of holly and mistletoe. Singing and gift giving were also part of these early pagan celebrations. Even a number of characteristics of St. Nicholas can be recognized in stories of the Norse God Odin or Wotan. According to myth, Odin, who wore a long, white beard, lived for most of the year in the far distant realm called Valhalla. Every December 21, accompanied by the spirits of the Viking heroes, Odin would sweep back to earth on his white horse and spirit away misbehaving children. The youngsters, perhaps in hopes of getting on his good side, would leave offerings of food for Odin's horse and his ghostly minions.

## Christmas and the Protestant Reformation

The changes in religious doctrine imposed during the Protestant Reformation of the 1500's are one important reason why there is such variety in the Christmas celebration of Switzerland. While the Catholic Church was content to adapt pre-Christian rites and ceremonies for Christian purposes, the reformers, including Ulrich Zwingli in Zurich and, later, John Calvin in Geneva, would have none of that. Among their objections to the Catholic expression of religion in general was its reliance on icons and symbols, which the reformers considered at best superstitious, and at worst, downright pagan. As Protestantism caught on in many parts of Swiss-German- and French-speaking Switzerland, various aspects of the Christmas celebration were suppressed by the new church. Even today, Christmas celebrations in regions of Switzerland that are chiefly Protestant tend to be quiet family affairs, while St. Nicholas celebrations and the more exuberant masking tend to occur chiefly in Catholic regions.

# Christmas at Home

Knowing that someone is Swiss does not necessarily reveal a lot about how he or she spends the winter holidays. Does the family celebration center around the nativity scene, or is the Christmas tree more important? Who brings the gifts—Father Christmas, Samichlaus, the *Christkindli, Père Noël,* the *Gesú Bambino*—and when does the gift-bearer arrive? In some ways the children of Switzerland are the luckiest in the world, because so many kind-hearted spirits stand ready to shower them with treats and presents during the holiday season.

Colorful glass ornaments depicting the symbols of Christmas hang from the boughs in many Swiss homes *(above)*. Adding the finishing touches to the Christmas tree, a Swiss family opts for the more traditional decorations of lighted candles and a star to top it off *(right)*.

Pages 16-17:
A cottage home in the canton of Graubünden glows with the spirit of Christmas.

As in much of the Christian West, Christmas is an important festival in Switzerland, accounting for seemingly endless hustle and bustle and preparation. The high point of the celebration takes place on Christmas Eve, when children are spirited out of the house or banished to a side room while their parents adorn the Christmas tree in secret.

The Swiss Christmas tree, unlike the American version, is often illuminated with real candles rather than strings of electric light bulbs. Gold and silver garlands twinkle on the branches, and multihued ornaments add color. Cookies, nuts, fruit, foil-wrapped chocolates, and small presents also hang from the boughs. A star representing the Star of Bethlehem often tops the tree, although some families prefer to reserve that spot for an angel, representing the Christkindli, a guardian angel thought to protect the household and/or the nativity scene. In fact, in some parts of Switzerland, it is the Christkindli who delivers the Christmas Eve presents.

Lots of eating, merrymaking, and visiting are also characteristic of Christmastime throughout Switzerland. The Swiss do not have a typical Christmas dinner that is enjoyed by most people, like turkey and dressing in the United States or roast goose in the United Kingdom. Instead, a number of dishes top the list of Swiss favorites. A longtime favorite is fondue, a mixture of any number of cheeses, most often Emmentaler (the "holey" cheese Americans know as Swiss cheese) and Gruyère; a shot of schnapps (kirsch); and white wine. Into this cheese sauce diners dip cubes of bread speared on long-handled forks. Increasing in popularity are two variations on fondue: *fondue chinoises* and *fondue bourguignonne,* in which pieces of beef are cooked in hot broth and hot oil, respectively. *Rösti,* a dish similar to hash browns, is served throughout Swiss-German-speaking Switzerland.

Many families enjoy a light meal on Christmas Eve, often consisting of cold cuts, vegetable salads, patés, and tarts. They then indulge in a fancy dinner at midday on December 25. Although Christmas Eve is usually a family affair, friends and relatives may gather on Christmas Day for a meal and hours of visiting and merrymaking.

Protestant and Catholic churches alike celebrate Christmas Eve midnight services, which are always well attended.

## St. Nicholas makes his rounds

In the Catholic areas of Switzerland, children mark the beginning of the Christmas season on December 6—St. Nicholas Day. Known as *Samichlaus* in the Swiss-German-speaking regions, *San Nicolao* among Italian-speakers, and *Père Noël* by those who speak French, St. Nicholas dons a few different guises. Sometimes he is

Donning an outfit much like that of the North American Santa Claus, St. Nicholas of Switzerland, along with his faithful friend, rests up for his day, December 6.

dressed in a red coat and sports a long white beard similar to the American Santa Claus. And sometimes he is dressed in his bishop's garb with a miter atop his head and a staff held firmly in his grip. His mode of transportation also varies. He may arrive either on foot or riding on a donkey. In Lugano in the canton of Ticino, St. Nicholas has even touched down in the *piazza*, or town square, in a helicopter!

Some communities arrange for St. Nicholas to appear in public places such as the town square or a department store. Sometimes, he even pays a visit to children's homes. When he arrives, mom or dad will often slip him a note outlining their children's offenses and accomplishments, so that he can scold or reward them appropriately. It is not unknown

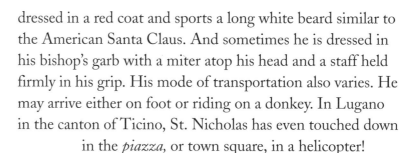

St. Nicholas happily greets his pint-sized admirers. But not far behind him is his frightful companion, Schmutzli, who awaits his chance to bundle up a naughty child *(left)*. The generous visitor delivers all kinds of Christmas goodies, including a variety of cookies, fruits, and nuts *(below)*.

for his frightful companion, Schmutzli, to bundle up a naughty child in his bag; but it is all in fun. Good little children sing a song or recite a poem for St. Nicholas, who rewards them with a bag of goodies. And as an added incentive to good behavior in the coming year, he may leave a bundle of switches tied with twine for mom and dad.

Those children who do not receive personal visits from St. Nicholas still benefit from his generosity. In some areas, youngsters leave their shoes outside and in the morning find them filled to the brim with all kinds of Christmas goodies.

## Christmas Swiss-German style

"Schöne Weihnachten" can be heard at Christmastime in the streets and homes of Switzerland's northern and central cantons, where Swiss-German is spoken. Specifically, this region consists of the cantons of Aargau, Bern, Glarus, Lucerne, St. Gallen, Schaffhausen, Schwyz, Solothurn, Thurgau, Uri, Zug, and Zurich; the half-cantons of Nidwalden, Obwalden, Basel-Land, Basel-Stadt, Ausser Rhoden, and Inner Rhoden; the eastern parts of the cantons of Fribourg and Valais; and much of the canton of Graubünden. The Swiss-German-speaking region also includes three of Switzerland's five major cities: Basel, Bern, and Zurich. The landscape of this region varies from the Jura Mountains in the northwest, across the rich farmland of the Swiss Plateau, to the mighty Swiss Alps.

In Swiss-German-speaking households, the Christmas season begins with the lighting of the first Advent candle on the fourth Sunday before Christmas. The family places an evergreen wreath decorated with small Christmas ornaments and four candles on the dining room table or a coffee table. The family gathers on each of the four Sundays of Advent to light one of the candles on the Advent wreath and sing Christmas carols. Lucky children may receive a little bag of nuts, tangerines, and other goodies. And parents and children have been known to take this opportunity to get in a few hours of *basteln*, or

Christmas means only one thing to some Swiss: cookies! And luckily there are always plenty to go around. Even the youngest bakers help in their preparation *(above)*. On the list of favorites are Tirggel *(below),* molded honey cookies that truly are edible works of art.

making handicrafts, such as nativity figures, straw Christmas ornaments, or candles.

Some Swiss children also have Advent calendars, with 24 little doors—one for every day in December up through Christmas Eve. On each day, they open a new door and are treated to a Christmas picture, or sometimes even a candy treat.

Swiss pastries are justifiably renowned, and *Weihnachtsguetzli,* or Christmas cookies molded into different shapes, are one of the centerpieces of the Swiss Christmas season. The Swiss-German-speaking regions lay claim to the most varied assortment and well-known of the Christmas cookies. Many cooks start baking early, a month or so before Christmas, to concoct the array of wonderful treats that will be enjoyed by the family and shared generously with friends and visitors. Shop windows also begin to fill with *Guetzli,* or cookies, packed in festive tins, boxes, and baskets.

*Läbchueche* (lasting cakes), *Läckerli* (little licks), and *Biberli* (little beavers) belong to a family of spiced honey-cookies related to the German *Lebkuchen*. Some Läbchueche are topped with little paper pictures called *Läbchuechebilder* with seasonal images such as Samichlaus, a Christmas tree, or a heart with an evergreen branch. Läckerli are flavored with orange peel, and Biberli are filled with a paste of ground almonds, lemon zest, and sometimes, kirsch.

*Änisbrötli*, little anise breads, start with anise-flavored dough pressed into molds carved with designs of Alpine flowers, such as edelweiss and gentian, or elaborate landscapes. These are similar to the traditional *Tirggel*, abundant in the Zurich area and said to be a descendant of ancient honey cakes offered as a sacrifice to the gods during pagan religious ceremonies. Many people so treasure the designs on Tirggel that instead of eating them, they hang them on their walls or the Christmas tree as decorations.

In a sweet shop, Swiss youngsters wonder how they might sink their teeth into a Läbchueche tower that stands twice their size.

Some popular Swiss cookies are associated with their place of origin. *Basler Brunsli* (Basel brownies) are spiced chocolate and hazelnut cookies often shaped as hearts. *Mailänderli,* named in honor of Milan, are golden sugar cookies traditionally cut into rounds and scored with parallel grooves. No spices compete with the rich flavor of butter and egg yolks. Other Guetzli are as noteworthy for their fanciful names as for their deliciousness. *Spitzbuebli,* or naughty boys, are shortbread jam-filled sandwich cookies dusted with powdered sugar. *Schenkeli,* crispy oblong fried cookies, get their name—lady's thighs—from their plump shape, as do *Totebeinli*—dead legs. Totebeinli are small, hard hazelnut bars that have been known to break teeth!

Children in Swiss-German-speaking Switzerland begin their preparations for Christmas early, making their gift requests to ensure a satisfying haul on Christmas Eve. Some children slip a note to St. Nicholas during his early December rounds. Others leave their lists on the windowsill for Christkindli to pick up during the night. The angel signals its receipt of the message by leaving a chocolate treat behind. The more practical children prefer to entrust their wish lists to the Swiss postal system. And for the children of certain cantons, if the timing is right, doing so may make someone very happy. For in four cantons and one half-canton—namely Valais, Solothurn, Bern, Lucerne, and Obwalden—there is a town of St. Niklaus, and a letter with a canceled stamp from one of these post offices on December 6 is a collector's item and a treasured keepsake.

All the preparations finally lead to Christmas Eve, generally the climax of the holiday celebration in Swiss-German-speaking Switzerland. On that evening, the Christmas tree in all its illuminated splendor, put up in carefully guarded secret by the parents, is revealed to the children. And at long last the eager youngsters are allowed to open their gifts.

Some families of the region choose to remember their departed loved ones on Christmas Eve by making a visit to

# Tasty Treats on the Bough

Through the centuries, chocolate has assumed a special place in Swiss life. This holds true even at Christmastime, when chocolate treats are given as gifts and used to decorate the home. Some merchants even sell colorful foil-wrapped chocolates molded in the shapes of the season and equipped with a small loop to make it easy to hang them on the Christmas tree.

Fine chocolate is as closely associated with Switzerland as fine watches and fine cheese. Switzerland may have risen to the world's premier supplier of chocolate because of three conditions: the Swiss sweet tooth, its long tradition of dairying, and its high standards of quality for everything it produces.

However, the Swiss did not invent chocolate—they only perfected it. The confection probably arrived in Switzerland in the final years of the 1600's, when Bürgermeister Heinrich Escher of Zurich returned home with the news of a delicious drink (an early version of hot cocoa) he had sampled in Brussels. The first Swiss chocolatier was François-Louis Cailler, who opened a chocolate factory in Vevey on the northeast shore of Lake Geneva in 1815. At that time and in the years to come, chocolate was consumed only as a beverage. That changed in 1847, when a British company discovered how to make solid "eating chocolate."

Sometime during this period, Rudolphe Lindt of Bern improved on the rather gritty, slightly bitter eating chocolate available at the time. He came up with a smooth, creamy chocolate that melted in the mouth. But the real breakthrough in chocolate came in Vevey in 1876 when Henri Nestlé teamed up with Daniel Peter, whose in-laws were the renowned chocolatiers, the Caillers. Peter devised a way to add condensed milk, which Nestlé had invented, to chocolate to make milk chocolate.

Today, the Swiss people are the world's largest consumers of chocolate, with a yearly per capita consumption of more than 20 pounds (10 kilograms). And while surely some of this munching does go on during the Christmas season, an array of Christmas cookies gives chocolate a run for its money during this festive time of year. At any rate, with the sweet, creamy treats dangling on the Christmas tree, no doubt in danger of melting in the warmth of dozens of candles, the urge to rescue the edible ornaments from a gooey demise must be great indeed!

the cemetery. There they place on the gravesites pine boughs or special arrangements that are sold especially for this occasion.

## Joyeux Noël: Christmas the French way

Geneva, Jura, Neuchâtel, Vaud, and most of Valais are the cantons that the French-speaking Swiss call home. The canton of Fribourg is bilingual, with two-thirds of its population speaking French and one-third speaking Swiss-German.

Unlike France itself, French-speaking Switzerland welcomed the church reforms of the 1500's, so this region, except for Fribourg, is overwhelmingly Protestant. Throughout most of the region, December 6 comes and goes without much notice. St. Nicholas's and Schmutzli's roles are played by Père Noël, or Father Christmas, and Père Fouettard, respectively. Père Noël climbs through the window on Christmas Eve to leave presents for good little boys and girls. With his red jacket lined with fur, white beard, and round tummy, Père Noël resembles the North American Santa Claus more than St. Nicholas does.

In some families, the children are treated to a personal visit from Père Noël. Before he hands out the presents, the children must display their talents by singing a song, reciting a poem, or playing an instrument. And lest the children forget the importance of good behavior throughout the year, Père Noël leaves behind a bundle of twigs bound with twine as a reminder of the consequences of being naughty.

In other households, Père Noël comes and goes on the sly. On Christmas Eve, the children are allowed in the living room to admire the tree, beautifully decorated but noticeably bare of presents. Then the children are ushered out again as the parents open the window to ease Père Noël's entrance. A little while later, the children are invited back into the living room, where their presents await them. Although Père Noël is no longer there, having slipped quickly out after doing his cheerful chore, the children are still required to put on a little performance before the present-opening can begin.

## Christmas in Ticino

Cross the Alps through the St. Gotthard Pass or the San
Bernardino Pass and there lies the canton of Ticino, where
many things are noticeably different. Here and there, palm
trees and mimosa replace pines and German and French give
way to Italian. In Christmas customs as well, there is a slight
shift in emphasis. Although most families put up a Christmas tree, it is the nativity scene, or *presepio*, that plays the
most cherished role in the celebration. The tree and the presepio generally go up at the same time. Out of storage comes
the little stable made of twigs or wood, and family members

Ticino, the southernmost
Swiss canton, is the warmest
part of the country. But even
here, snow occasionally
graces the branches of the
native palm trees.

embark on outdoor expeditions for moss to line the manger. When that is done, they place figurines of the Madonna, Giuseppe (Joseph), and the sheep, mules, and other animal guardians. Children sometimes make angels at school during holiday time, and those take their place in the presepio as well. Now all is ready for the arrival of the Gesú Bambino, the baby Jesus, whom the family will lovingly add to the presepio at midnight on Christmas Eve.

The presepio, or nativity scene, is the centerpiece of the Ticinese Christmas celebration. Most churches of this Italian-speaking canton display a presepio in which each figure is carefully placed around the Gesú Bambino, or baby Jesus.

The churches of Ticino all display presepios, too. In some parishes, it is traditional for teen-agers to collect the moss and other adornments and assemble the presepio. In others, the priests take on this important task.

St. Nicholas is San Nicolao in Italian-speaking Switzerland, and he makes his usual rounds, handing out small goodies on December 6. But the children of Ticino receive their special presents on Christmas Day, and many believe that it is the Gesú Bambino who leaves them. Some thoughtful children put out a bowl of milk or other refreshment for him before they go to bed on Christmas Eve.

The Ticinese enjoy their main Christmas meal on the afternoon of Christmas Day. Italian specialties such as *polenta*, a corn-meal mush; a braised beef dish called *brazatto*; and *risotto*, a rice dish, in a variety of forms are among the favorites.

## Holiday in Graubünden

*Quaida not, sencha not*
*regna pôs dapertuot.*
*Be a Bethlehem vagliand*
*staun ils genituors urand*
*sper luch cher iffaunt.*

"Silent Night" is as cherished a carol in the Romansh-speaking mountain valleys of Graubünden as it is throughout the rest of Switzerland. The words just sound strangely exotic when sung in this ancient tongue. And Switzerland's largest canton is delightfully unique in other ways. Although Graubünden's towering peaks are the setting for some of the world's most glamorous skiing at resorts such as St. Moritz, Davos, Klosters, Arosa, and Pontresina, most of its inhabitants are down-to-earth, small-town folk and farmers who keep to their traditional ways. The mountains and pine forests of Graubünden are famous in another way: The landscape that inspired the beloved children's tale *Heidi* was the mountainsides above the small town of Maienfeld in the north.

The Engadine Valley in the far eastern part of the canton is the heart of Romansh-speaking Switzerland. At Christmastime, evergreen branches spill from the windowsills of the traditional houses—stout stuccoed homes of several stories with heavy, wooden, arched Etruscan-style doorways—and gold ribbons decorate the wrought-iron door handles. Many of these old houses are covered with designs in an ancient style of etching known as *sgraffito*. Sgraffito

Graubünden, Switzerland's largest canton, is unique in many ways. Majestic snow-capped mountains serve as the backdrop to traditional homes that are often decorated with sgraffito etching.

designs are made by coating dark gray stucco with a layer of whitewash and then scratching away the whitewash so the dark underlayer shows through. Some houses list all their inhabitants—sometimes spanning 300 years. Others are decorated with rosettes, pinwheels, braided ropes, and other abstract patterns.

Graubünden is perhaps the single most diverse canton in a country known for its diversity. Romansh, whose several dialects are spoken by about a third of Graubündners, is only one of the canton's native languages. In the north, which borders on Austria and Liechtenstein, the people speak Swiss-German. The region on the south and east, cradled by Italy, is home to Italian speakers.

Graubünden's Christmas traditions reflect this diversity. Some children wake up on Christmas morning to discover their presents from the Christkindli, who visits on Christmas Eve. Others enjoy a visit from St. Nicholas and Schmutzli on December 6, as well. In Catholic towns, St. Nicholas comes dressed as a bishop, while in Protestant towns, he is called *Sontgaclau* and bears the terrifying image associated with Schmutzli elsewhere. Children often receive presents from aunts, uncles, and other relatives on Christmas Day.

As in Ticino, most of the families of Graubünden decorate with both a Christmas tree and a nativity scene, which is known here as a *purseppen*. Each family prepares its own traditional menu for the Christmas meal, often featuring ham or the regional specialty, *Bündnerfleisch*—air-dried beef pressed into rectangular loaves and served in paper-thin slices.

Hospitality reigns supreme at holiday time in Graubünden, as in other regions of Switzerland. In Graubünden homes, guests are always greeted with a bowl of Christmas treats, including *Churer Zimmetstern*, star-shaped cinnamon cookies with a sweet meringue glaze that originated in Graubünden's capital of Chur and hard, white cookies called *Anischräbeli*.

There is an ancient custom in Poschiavino called the "Christmas-rose watch." A group of women friends gath-

ers at one house, where the hostess has decorated her table with the prettiest tablecloth she owns. On the table are many burning candles and a beautiful vase filled with water. In the vase is a plant that looks like a flower bulb surrounded by a mass of fibers. The women start to sing hymns and carols. From time to time, one of them stands up and looks into the vessel. After a time, their voices begin to get hoarse, but still they keep on singing. Finally, around midnight, the plant in the vase has absorbed enough water that it begins to look like a flower with oblong leaves. One of the women announces, "The Christmas rose has opened!" Then they sing a joyful carol.

The strange plant that marks the dawn of Christmas Day is a type of rose of Jericho native to the Arabian peninsula. When the plant wilts, it draws up into a nest-like mass. When it is soaked in water, it swells up again. Early Christian monks regarded this phenomenon as a miracle of rebirth brought on by the special powers of the holy sites in that part of the world.

With joy in their voices and warmth in their hearts, carolers in the canton of Graubünden gather around the Christmas tree to rejoice in the spirit of Christmas. For sharing the songs of the season, many Swiss carolers are offered Churer Zimmet-stern, star-shaped cinnamon cookies.

# Country Christmas, City Christmas

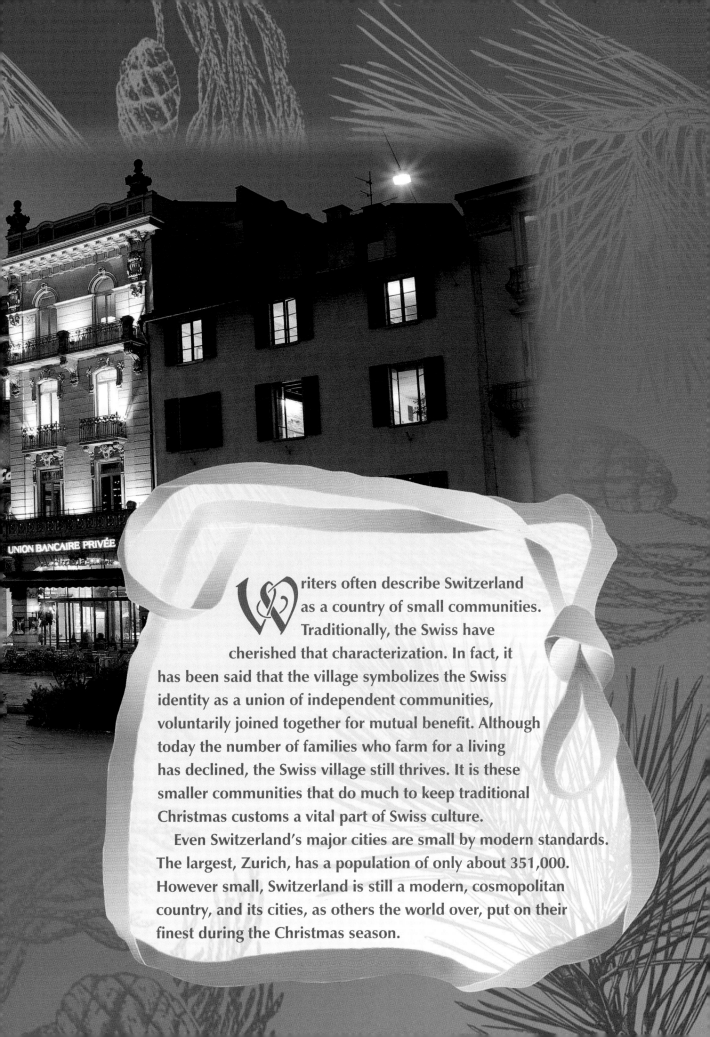

Writers often describe Switzerland as a country of small communities. Traditionally, the Swiss have cherished that characterization. In fact, it has been said that the village symbolizes the Swiss identity as a union of independent communities, voluntarily joined together for mutual benefit. Although today the number of families who farm for a living has declined, the Swiss village still thrives. It is these smaller communities that do much to keep traditional Christmas customs a vital part of Swiss culture.

Even Switzerland's major cities are small by modern standards. The largest, Zurich, has a population of only about 351,000. However small, Switzerland is still a modern, cosmopolitan country, and its cities, as others the world over, put on their finest during the Christmas season.

## Quaint Country Customs

Like nearly every other aspect of Swiss identity, there is no "typical" Swiss village. In the Berner Oberland in central Switzerland, farm families, their hired help, and their cows live in large, slope-roofed farmhouses. Ticinese village homes are made of stones of granite, and in the wine-making region around Lake Geneva, the villages are nestled among sweeping vineyards.

Christmas is especially meaningful in Swiss rural areas— especially in the mountain villages—for Christmas church services are often one of the few times during the year that the whole community gathers. The mountain-dwellers descend from the snowy slopes, some on foot, others on skis, still others on sleds drawn by horses jangling with bells. These Christmas gatherings offer an opportunity for families to settle conflicts with a joyous public reconciliation.

Perhaps so moved by these church services, a Swiss composer by the name of Paul Burkhard wrote a beautiful play for the church in his home village of Zell, a small community near Zurich. The play, entitled *D'Zäller Wiehnacht (A Swiss Nativity)*, is performed hundreds of times in several different places each year. The song that is perhaps the best-known Swiss Christmas carol—"Das ist der Stern"—comes from this play.

In the rural communities of Switzerland, people once held to old Christmas superstitions. For example, on Christmas Eve the woman in the family would pick the most perfect onion from the larder. She would cut that onion in half and remove 12 cuplike sections, which she would fill with salt. She would then line them up to represent the 12 months of the year. In the morning, the family could see what the coming year's weather would be: The onion sections containing dry salt foretold dry months, while those with damp salt showed which months would be rainy.

Other folk superstitions concerned farm animals, which were supposed to attain the ability to speak for one hour on Christmas Eve before the clock struck midnight. People avoided their farm animals during this hour, because disaster or even death was the fate of the human eavesdropper.

Pages 30-31:
The streets of Lugano glimmer like gold during the season of Christmas.

Clipping the wings of chickens on Christmas Eve, according to those with a superstitious mind, kept them out of harm's way from foxes and other predators all year long. And tying straw around all the fruit trees during Christmas week was said to ensure a plentiful harvest the next year.

Brave souls who wanted to know how many more years they would live could find out on Christmas Eve by opening a Bible at random and pointing to a chapter. The number of verses in the chapter told them the number of years they had left. And young people liked to safeguard their chances for future marital bliss by drinking from nine different fountains in their village as the Christmas Eve

The church is at the heart of Christmas in small Swiss villages, where whole communities gather together. Many parishes reenact the long journey of Mary and Joseph for the enjoyment of townspeople.

church bells rang. When they finished this ritual, they hurried to the church steps, where, it is said, their future spouse would be waiting.

## Celebrating St. Nick

The celebration of St. Nicholas Day takes on a different form in the streets of Switzerland's towns and villages than it does in the homes. In various communities throughout Swiss-German-speaking Switzerland, the holiday brings out the pagan in everybody. People don elaborate head-dresses and masks and hoist giant bells to pay noisy homage to the beloved saint.

Dressed in white robes, participants in the celebration of Klausjagen fill the streets of Küssnacht, a village in the canton of Schwyz. A traditional part of the celebration are huge bishop's miters, called Iffele, that are illuminated by candles. The towering headpieces provide spectacular sights of light and color.

The village of Küssnacht in the canton of Schwyz puts on a well-known celebration called *Klausjagen,* or the pursuit of St. Nicholas, on the evening of December 5. Hundreds of participants dress in white bishop's robes and wear huge bishop's miters, called *Iffele,* constructed of heavy cardboard. Abstract decorative patterns—rosettes, stars, crosses—are cut into the miters, and the holes are covered with colored tissue paper. Candles burn inside the towering headpieces, making a beautiful display of color and light reminiscent of stained-glass windows. While smoking small, crooked cigars, a small group of paraders blows horns while larger groups—sometimes including hundreds of participants—ring huge cowbells, which they swing from thigh to thigh. A crew of *Geisselchlepfer,* or whip-crackers, adds to the noise. These men and boys crack long whips in rhythmic unison. The deafening din is sure to banish any evil spirit lurking in the village streets for the year to come.

The people of Hallwil, in the canton of Aargau, put on a similar show, which they call the *Chlauswettchlöpfe,* a St. Nicholas Day whip-cracking contest. Winners are awarded a pewter pitcher, and six qualified crackers—boys 13 or 14 years old—get to take part in the *Chlausjage* the next day. The six play the part of spirits who visit homes to reward the well-behaved children with gifts and warn the naughty children that they had better shape up.

In the Zurich suburb of Wollishofen, a red-coated St. Nicholas leads a parade of teen-agers called *Wollishofer Kläuse* (Nicholases of Wollishofen). Like their kindred spirits in Küssnacht, the Wollishofer Kläuse wear white robes and headdresses illuminated with candles.

Children are responsible for the St. Nicholas procession in the villages of the canton of Glarus. Each village has its own particular style of celebrating the *Klausschellen,* or ringing of cowbells for St. Nicholas. But generally speaking, the custom involves going out sometime during a day or evening around December 6, ringing the ever-popular giant cowbells, and begging for treats door-to-door. This custom is said to have originated in the 1700's, when the

# A Swiss Pilgrimage

Einsiedeln, situated in a valley of the Alps between Lake Zurich and Lake Lucerne, has been a center for pilgrimages for more than a thousand years. What causes people of all ages and from all over the world to journey to this small village in the canton of Schwyz? A carved wooden image of the Black Madonna.

The Benedictine monastery of Einsiedeln was founded in the A.D. 800's when Meinrad, a monk, chose this place to pursue his devotions in solitude. The abbess of Zurich gave him a picture of the Virgin Mother, for which Meinrad quickly built a chapel. The story has it that when Meinrad was murdered in A.D. 861 by thieves, two ravens, who had been assisting Meinrad, followed the treasure-seekers to Zurich and shrieked over their heads until they were caught. Soon a monastery was built over Meinrad's grave, and as the ceremony to consecrate the monastery began, a voice was heard. It said three times,

"Brother, desist: God himself has consecrated this building."

Over the years the monastery of Einsiedeln was destroyed five times by fire, but the Black Madonna was always rescued unharmed. When pilgrimages to the wooden image peaked in the 1600's and 1700's, construction of the present-day beautiful baroque church and monastery area began. Today the buildings are considered to be among the finest examples of baroque architecture in Switzerland. The Black Madonna is kept in the Gnadenkapple (chapel of Grace), a black marble chapel inside the church.

Even today Einsiedeln remains a focus for religion and culture. While pilgrimages are still popular the year around, many people make their journey in winter to view the Bethlehem Diorama, a representation of the manger in Bethlehem with 500 carved wooden figures, that stands near the square outside the abbey.

Einsiedeln in the canton of Schwyz is home to the Bethlehem Diorama, a wooden representation of the Nativity scene. Each year the diorama attracts hundreds of tourists during the Christmas season.

first big industries were emerging and children of working-class families were allowed to beg for handouts at Christmastime. Today, it is all in fun, and any child, regardless of the family's economic status, can join the festivities.

The city of Fribourg puts on a special St. Nicholas Day celebration with a slightly more cosmopolitan flair. Fribourg, nestled on the bluffs above the Sarine River, is an ancient city on the frontier between Swiss-German- and French-speaking Switzerland. As such, it is a truly bilingual city, with street signs in both Swiss-German and French and a population generally fluent in both tongues. During the 1500's, Fribourg also remained firmly Catholic, while the rest of the region went the way of Calvin and the other Protestant reformers.

St. Nicholas (or Père Noël in French), astride his donkey and accompanied by his sidekick Schmutzli (or Père Fouettard), leads a procession through the streets of the old city. As he makes his way, he greets the children and hands out nuts, tangerines, and *Biscômes*, spiced buns in the shape of St. Nicholas. Eventually he arrives at a raised stage erected in front of the Cathédral St. Nicholas. There he addresses the crowd with a humorous summarization, in both French and German, of the local events of the past year.

Visitors to the winter sport centers of Switzerland have been known to take part in the fine art of ice sculpture. The results are as grand as the artisans' imaginations, as evidenced by this giant frozen kangaroo.

## Holy Night celebrations

St. Nicholas Day is for boys in Hallwil, but on Christmas Eve and Christmas Day, seven 13- to 14-year-old girls play the starring roles. One girl, dressed all in white and her face hidden by a veil, impersonates the Christmas Child, or *Wienechtchind*. Accompanied by six attendants wearing rose-colored robes, the Wienechtchind visits as many homes in the village as time allows, silently greeting the families inside with a handshake and passing out treats to the children. After the six attendants sing a carol, the group silently departs.

In remembrance of the plague of 1348, members of the Brotherhood of St. Sebastian in the town of Rheinfelden participate in the Brunnensingen, or fountain-singing. Tall black hats are part of the traditional attire for this solemn occasion.

Another somewhat solemn Christmas Eve celebration takes place in Rheinfelden, a town east of Basel on the Rhine. There, 12 members of the Brotherhood of St. Sebastian participate in the *Brunnensingen* (fountain-singing), a procession that has taken place since 1541 in remembrance of the plague of 1348. Dressed in somber funeral attire and wearing tall black hats, the 12 visit seven fountains in turn. At each fountain, they sing a carol, pausing when God or Christ is mentioned in the song to doff their hats in praise. When they have finished their circuit, they attend midnight Mass together.

Another Christmas Eve procession that involves men in hats takes place in Ziefen in the canton of Basel. The *Nünichlingler* is so called because it involves the ringing of bells (*chlingle*) at 9 p.m. (*nüni*). Thirty or more young (and until recently, only unmarried) men dress up in dark coats and wear towering black top hats. Without saying a word, they proceed with dignity through the town, ringing their bells rhythmically. The tallest man in the group wears a white beard and leads the parade, representing a mean-spirited Samichlaus. He carries a long pole from the end of which a sooty rag dangles. Until the 1950's, the man used the rag to frighten and anger people by smearing soot on them and their houses and scaring away winter demons. Today this curious display is a playful and harmless competition among those in attendance.

## City celebrations

Swiss cities all have their own special charm. Bern, the capital, has its nearly 600-year-old sandstone arcades that stretch for miles; Zurich, wealthy, sophisticated, and glittering, boasts lovely views of Lake Zurich and the Limmat River; Geneva appears chic yet proper on the shore of Lake Geneva; Basel, historically a center of culture and learning, but also a busy port on the Rhine River, receives thousands of international commuters each day; and Lugano, with its Mediterranean flair, shows off its mountain landscape, palm trees, and blooming gardens.

Many cities throughout the world put on their holiday finest at Christmastime, and Swiss cities are no exception. For example, Zurich's Bahnhofstrasse, considered one of Europe's most fashionable shopping districts, is ablaze with lights hung in long vertical strands that cascade over the streets like drapery, suggesting the glow of the northern lights. The bridges

Metal trees aglow with Christmas lights branch out over the Limmat River in the city of Zurich.

Zurich's Bahnhofstrasse, considered one of Europe's most fashionable shopping districts, lives up to its reputation, especially at Christmastime. Strands upon strands of tiny lights cascade over the streets, while the hustle and bustle of the season takes place below.

on the Limmat River are decorated with metal trees. Each branch is tipped by a light, giving an effect akin to a glowing starburst. Towering evergreens in city squares shine with colored lights. Most cities also hold Christmas markets, where a seemingly endless assortment of Christmas decorations—and the raw materials for making them—are for sale.

As as a special treat for the children, the cities of Zurich, Bern, and Basel all have a *Weihnachtstram* or *Märlitram.* The gaily lit antique trolley cars conducted by Samichlaus roll through the main streets, while the young passengers listen to fairy tales. Rides are free or may be sponsored by local stores.

The streets of Swiss towns are also warmed by the joyful sound of caroling. Swiss-German-speaking Lucerne, Rapperswil, and Wettingen have the best-known gatherings of *Sternsinger*, or star singers, who proceed through the streets during Advent carrying illuminated stars representing the Star of Bethlehem. Accompanying the singers are the Three Wise Men and Mary, Jesus, and Joseph. The canton of Graubünden has a rich tradition of holiday singing. In Romansh-speaking communities such as Celerina and Samedan in the Engadine Valley, adults and children start caroling around five o'clock on Christmas Eve. Later in the evening, teen-agers carrying candles lend their voices to the choir.

Good works also add to the holiday glow of Swiss cities. Every Christmas Eve in Zurich, Ernst Sieber, a popular minister, author, charity leader, and government official, organizes a special meal for drug addicts and the poor. In Geneva, the Women's Guild of the United Nations sponsors an international Christmas bazaar at the Palais des Nations, the European UN headquarters. Volunteers sell Christmas crafts and food from around the world, and a portion of the proceeds is donated to charity.

All aboard! A gaily lit antique trolley car, known as a Marlitram, rolls around the streets of some of Switzerland's largest cities during the holiday season. Much to the delight of children, Samichlaus himself serves as conductor. This particular trolley makes the rounds of the Zurich shopping district of Bahnhofstrasse.

In Basel, Bern, and other Swiss cities, a service that began in 1990 to help save lives has been quite successful. Organized by the nonprofit group *Opération Nez Rouge* (Operation Red Nose, named for its reindeer emblem), which originated in Quebec, Canada, the service provides rides to those who have celebrated the winter holidays with just a little too much enthusiasm. Volunteer drivers see to it that people and their cars make it home safe and sound. The goal of the service is to prevent car accidents, so that all may enjoy the holiday season.

Behind an unassuming façade at 14 Spalenberg Street in Basel's medieval old town, the Johann Wanner Christmas House is jammed with Christmas trinkets and supplies of all kinds.

And radio campaigns in various areas urge folks to invite single or lonely people to their Christmas celebrations or to transport disabled people to their holiday destinations.

## Shopping for Christmas

Shopping is just as much a part of Christmas as eating and merrymaking. And there are plenty of shops in the cities of Switzerland in which to find that perfect gift, buy decorations, or simply take in the sights and smells of all that the merchants have to offer.

Basel, located in the far northwest corner of Switzerland on the borders of France and Germany and divided by the Rhine River, is home to a couple of well-known shops that are open the year around, but whose wares are most appropriate at Christmastime.

The first is the Johann Wanner Christmas House, which is perhaps best known for its impressive assortment of glass Christmas ornaments. Located in Basel's medieval old town, the store is jammed with Christmas trinkets and supplies of all kinds, including cards, lights, tinsel, strings of beads, chocolates for hanging on the tree, and miniature toys. Dozens of trees, decked out in color-coordinated decorations or thematically related baubles, such as farm animals, musical instruments, or shimmering fish, line the narrow aisles and hang from the ceiling. But the shop's real claim to fame is the glass ornaments, which are available in dozens of shapes, from traditional angels, Santas, and stars, to more unique old-time radios, monkeys riding bikes, airplanes, dice, castles, and clowns.

Also in Basel is the famous Läckerli-Huus (Leckerli House). While a variety of sweets and other gifts can be bought here, the shop, as its name implies, features the local specialty—Leckerli, a chewy spiced cookie of almond, honey, dried fruit, and kirsch. This cookie, sure to please any sweet tooth, has been made in Basel since the 1300's, when sugar was still unknown in Europe. And the proprietors of Läckerli-Huus boast that they have not changed their recipe since those days of more than 600 years ago. At Christmastime, Läckerli-Huus also sells Hypokras, a spiced wine that is especially popular with Basel residents during the holidays. In addition to its renowned goodies, the shop carries an impressive line of decorative canisters and other truly Swiss gifts. But if the Leckerli and other gifts do not attract the passers-by during the Christmas holiday season, the storefront surely does. Toward the end of November, Läckerli-Huus joins other merchants in bedecking its shop with colorful lights and fanciful decorations.

During the Christmas season the city of Zurich hosts a number of events where merchants show off their goods to eager shoppers. Near the city square of Bürkliplatz, the Zurich Advent Magic is held between December 1 and 6. The "magic" lies in the many Advent Ships afloat the Limmat. Each ship houses a different shop. For example, there

# Escalade

Ask a Genevan how Christmas is celebrated in that city, and the reply may be a dignified, "Christmas here is a quiet, private affair. We don't make a big ruckus. After all, the Reformation put an end to a lot of unnecessary religious fuss." True enough, the Protestant Reformation caught on like a brushfire with Calvin's inspired preaching at Cathèdrale-St-Pierre, and even today, the stripped-down Puritan simplicity of the now-Protestant church is a fitting symbol for the Genevan distaste for anything too rollicking.

Except, of course, for Escalade.

The *Escalade* (French for "scaling the walls"), comes right in the middle of the holiday season, on December 11. And the celebration, which usually lasts an entire weekend, is filled to the brim with history and local pride. During the celebration the town becomes both the site of a live-action history lesson and a great big party. Included in the events are reenactments of the scaling of the old city walls, demonstrations of period weapons, and singing by children dressed in costume. The celebration culminates with Genevans pouring noisily into the streets to celebrate the

## Escalade Marzipan Vegetables

7 oz. almond paste*
3 tbsp. light corn syrup
1/2 tsp. vanilla extract
1 - 1-3/4 cups  sifted confectioners' sugar, separated
food coloring

Place almond paste in a medium mixing bowl. Using a fork, break up almond paste into small pieces. Add corn syrup and vanilla extract; mix thoroughly. Add 3/4 cup of the powdered sugar, 1/4 cup at a time, until mixture forms a smooth, stiff dough. Continue adding powdered sugar a little at a time, kneading dough until it is no longer sticky. Color and shape small balls of marzipan into vegetables or other figures as desired.

* Available in the baking section of most grocery stores

Genevans dressed in period costume take to the streets in mid-December to celebrate Escalade, which recognizes the defeat in 1602 of the French Duke of Savoy. The festivities culminate at St. Pierre, where participants gather in the glow of a bonfire and rejoice in song. To the children of Geneva, the best part of this happy occasion is the three-legged, chocolate marmite— or soup kettle—filled to the brim with marzipan vegetables.

Although the realistic battle reenactments are true crowd-pleasers, one of the highlights of the occasion, especially for the children, is the three-legged *marmites,* or soup kettles, made of chocolate and filled with marzipan vegetables. No good Genevan home is without one at this time of year. The marmite plays a major part in the Escalade celebration because, as the story goes, when the Savoyard soldiers were making their assault on the city walls, a housewife, Mère Royaume, leaned out the window and dumped a pot of steaming soup on the attackers. She then heaved the pot onto the head of one, killing him. Her quick thinking raised the alarm that the city was under attack. And while each family celebrates in its own way, traditionally after the Saturday-night family dinner during Escalade, the youngest person present smashes the chocolate marmite, declaring *"Ainsi périssent les ennemis de la République!"* ("Thus perish the enemies of the Republic!").

defeat in 1602 of the French Duke of Savoy, whose lineage had ruled Geneva for many generations and who was trying to recapture the city and turn it back to Catholicism. Dressed in period costume and bearing torches, Genevans proceed through the city streets accompanied by a herald on horseback, who pauses from time to time to proclaim the Genevans' victory over the Savoyards. The celebration ends at St. Pierre, where the happy paraders sing patriotic songs and bask in the glow of a large bonfire.

is a restaurant ship, a linen ship, a pin ship, and a hobby ship. Aside from the shopping, a number of shows enliven the event, including strolling clowns who have been known to invade the ships and entertain unsuspecting browsers. For the children there is a Fairy-Tale Island. Youngsters and their parents alike can enjoy games, contests with prizes, and other entertainment while waiting for a visit from Father Christmas, who upon his arrival hands out pins, nuts, and candies to all children in attendance.

St. Andrew's Church in Zurich, where services are held in English, is the stage for the grand annual St. Andrew's Bazaar. The bazaar showcases Christmas gifts, groceries, cakes, books, toys, and an assortment of handicrafts. Also in Zurich is the Christmas Collectors' Fair, which boasts thousands of Christmas antiques, art works, second-hand items, and collectibles shown by more than 800 exhibitors. There is even a special hall reserved solely for model trains.

And finally, in Zurich's old town, Niederdorf, stands Cafe

Shopkeepers in Zurich dress their windows for the season, much to the enjoyment of shoppers who busily hunt for those perfect gifts.

The famous Cafe Schober in Zurich's old town of Niederdorf offers seasonal confections that are as pleasing to the eye as they are to the palate.

Schober. The building that houses this cafe was erected in 1340, and the cafe itself has been in business more than 100 years. While always a pleasant place to shop and enjoy a steaming cup of hot chocolate and a pastry, Cafe Schober is the place to go for the nostalgia of Christmas. At this time of year, the cafe exhibits its eye-catching *Haxenhauser*, or Witch's House. The house is made of chocolate, gingerbread, and candy trimmings. Every part of the house is edible, except the dolls of the Witch and Hansel and Gretel. In addition to this mouth-watering display, Cafe Schober is a popular place for buying gifts for those with a sweet tooth.

# Celebrating the New Year and Other Holiday Traditions

Although Christmas is the focus of the winter holiday season, celebrating the New Year brings many Swiss to the streets in wild pageants of tradition and fun. The winter holiday season also includes a number of festivals that commemorate the harvest and the coming of winter. For example, November brings harvest festivals such as Bern's onion market and the beet festival in Richterswil. The holiday season comes to a close with the celebration of the feast of the Epiphany on January 6, commemorating the arrival of the Three Wise Men in Bethlehem to pay their respects to the infant Jesus.

New Year's Eve is often called *Silvester* in Swiss-German-speaking Switzerland, as it is the feast day of St. Silvester. And in certain areas of Switzerland, the New Year arrives twice—on January 1 and again on January 13. The extra New Year's Day is a throwback to the days when people followed the Julian calendar, which was adopted in 46 B.C. by Julius Caesar and used throughout the Western world for more than 1,500 years. But after all that time, it had lost step with the solar year. To bring the calendar back in line, Pope Gregory instituted the Gregorian calendar, the one we use today. But certain Protestant areas of Europe, including some villages in the east of Switzerland, refused to adopt the Gregorian calendar, instead clinging to the old Julian calendar for centuries. As a result, these villages acknowledge the New Silvester on December 31, and the Old Silvester on January 12.

In the city of Zurich, schoolchildren celebrate yet another Silvester—School Silvester. This Silvester comes a bit earlier than the others, occurring on the last day of school before Christmas break. On this day, the children awaken very early and hit the streets running. They set off fireworks, ring cow bells, and hit pan lids together as cymbals, all in an effort to make as much noise as they possibly can.

## New Year's customs

Whenever the Swiss celebrate it, New Year's is a festive time in Switzerland. In the fashionable ski resorts such as Gstaad and St. Moritz, jet-set parties make it a glittering, high-class affair, while joyful processions of torchbearing skiers winding down the slopes add an unmatched beauty to the celebration. In cities, people celebrate in restaurants or at parties, while in rural areas bonfires burn. In Geneva, people gather at the Cathédral-St-Pierre to hear *la Clemence*, the famous centuries-old bell pealing in the New Year. After midnight, people wish one another well and dance in the square.

Many families celebrate New Year's Day with another

Pages 48-49:
Winter brings not only the celebration of Christmas but many other traditions, including excursions to the sports centers of Switzerland, such as St. Moritz in the canton of Graubünden.

special feast, often featuring the traditional New Year's loaf called *Birewegge,* or pear roll, a sweet dough filled with a dark filling of dried pears and spices. Many people visit their friends and neighbors, showing up with a jug of *Hypokras,* a mulled combination of red and white wines, spices, sugar, and cloves named after the father of medicine, Hippocrates.

Special breads are traditional New Year's treats. A braided bread called *Zopf* is quite popular. Some residents of the half-canton of Nidwalden in central Switzerland may serve a spiced dough sweetened with honey and filled with gingerbread and candied citrus rind. The New Year's bread typical of the canton of Thurgau is a puff pastry with an apple-and-raisin filling. And in the valley of the Rhine River in northern Switzerland, bakers proudly present a loaf brimming with ground hazelnuts, dried fruit, and honey.

The Swiss New Year's celebration would not be complete without the tasty Birewegge, or pear roll.

# Harvest Festivals

In Switzerland, the coming of winter is anticipated with a number of festivals that take place in November. There are the *Gansabhauet,* in the community of Sursee, in the canton of Lucerne; the *Räbechilbi* in Richterswil, in the canton of Zurich; and the best-known of the three, the *Zibelemärit* in Bern.

The people of Sursee celebrate November 11, the Feast of Saint Martin, with an unusual game called the *Gansabhauet,* roughly translated as "chopping the goose." Dressed in a red robe, sporting a large sun-shaped mask, blindfolded, and wielding a somewhat blunt sword, young Surseeans compete to see who can chop down a dead goose suspended from a wire in the town square. The contestants are accompanied by drummers dressed in striking black-and-yellow costumes, whose job is both to lead them to their quarry and confuse them at the same time. The game is watched by a large crowd, who heckle the participants good-naturedly as they grope and chop away at the hapless goose. Between contestants, younger children take part in sack races, tree-climbing contests, and ugly-face competitions.

The origin of the Gansabhauet itself is unknown, but it may be

The second Saturday in November finds the townspeople of Richterswil in the canton of Zurich celebrating the Räbechilbi. The trademarks of this occasion are bright, beautiful lanterns made from hollowed beets. Here they illuminate decorative houses used in the procession.

Most onions bring tears to people's eyes, but not these happy bulbs found hanging around Bern's Zibelemärit, or onion market. Hundreds of farmers take part in the open-air market held on the fourth Monday of November.

related to the custom of honoring St. Martin, one of the patron saints of Switzerland, by offering up a fine, fat goose as a tithe. The first recorded mention of the custom occurred in 1821, though it had been going on for much longer. The children's games became part of the event in 1880.

On the second Saturday in November, in the town of Richterswil on the shore of Lake Zurich, about a thousand people of all ages take part in the Räbechilbi, a procession through the streets illuminated only by lanterns made of hollowed beets. A group of black-clad women leads the procession. One of several such beet-processions in Swiss-German-speaking Switzerland, the Räbechilbi has been celebrated since the 1920's. According to tradition, its roots go back to 1850, when a group of women led the way to the evening church service with their beet-lanterns.

The fourth Monday of the month of November brings the Zibelemärit, or onion market, to Bern. At hundreds of stalls, local farmers sell their winter vegetables and nuts and especially their onions: braided into ropes, painted like the face of a clock, and fashioned into onion dolls and other novelties. It is a chance for households to lay in a supply of onions for the winter and to enjoy themselves watching schoolchildren cavort in onion costumes, wage confetti battles, and perform satirical sketches. The Zibelemärit has been around since the 1400's, but how it evolved into its present form is unclear. According to a popular account, the market originated in 1405 after a devastating fire destroyed the city. The city of Fribourg sent 100 workers to help the Bernese rebuild their city. In appreciation, Bern granted the farmers of Fribourg the right to sell their only product, onions, at an open-air market.

Schoolboys await their cue to begin the "downhill ringing of large bells," or Achetringele, on New Year's Eve in Laupen in the canton of Bern.

## New Year's processions

The Swiss fondness for boisterous displays on their festival days extends, of course, to the celebration of the New Year. Some of the most colorful and unusual New Year's customs take place in the community of Laupen in the canton of Bern, in the St. Gallen village of Wil, and in Urnäsch and other communities in the canton of Appenzell.

On New Year's Eve in Laupen, schoolboys gather at the castle, excited for the start of the *Achetringele*, roughly translated as the "downhill ringing of large bells." Some of the boys, equipped with large bells, are the Achetringele themselves. Others take the role of *Bäsemanne*, or "broom men," and carry long poles festooned with juniper branches. But perhaps the luckiest of all are the *Blaateremannli*, "bladder men," who carry bouquets of pigs' bladders inflated with air. Thus outfitted, the boys set off for the town center. Along the way, the leader of the procession greets spectators with friendly rhyming wishes for a happy New Year, while the broom men wave their brooms. When the procession has ended, the real fun begins as the paraders begin to pummel the onlookers with the pigs' bladders, paying special attention to the young girls.

This custom originated in the early 1800's, at which time it took place on Christmas. No one knows for sure the origins of the specific roles. But because of its rowdy, irreverent character, church and town officials tried unsuccessfully to have it banned. Instead, the date was switched to New Year's Eve.

Another New Year's procession, the *Silvesterumzug* of Wil, originated in the statutory lantern inspection required long ago. At that time, officials, accompanied by lantern bearers, would inspect all houses for emergency lighting every New Year's Eve. Nowadays, at six o'clock

Dressed as "bladder men," these participants in the New Year's tradition of Achetringele carry bouquets of pigs' bladders inflated with air. Unsuspecting spectators beware: The celebration culminates with the bladders being hurled into the crowd of onlookers.

in the evening, the lights of the town are turned down and hundreds of children play the role of the lantern bearers. Attended by drummers, the children proceed through the town carrying homemade lanterns. They stop three times to sing carols with accompaniment by the town band. At the end of the evening, each participating child receives a pastry. The next evening, judges award prizes to the best lanterns.

In the Aargau village of Hallwil, the people celebrate New Year's Eve with a custom that touchingly combines pagan noisemaking with Christian reverence. On the hill overlooking the village, in the orange glow of a huge bonfire, the villagers gather. At 10 minutes before midnight, eight men begin to beat rhythmically on a threshing board, an old-fashioned tool used to separate grain from chaff. Seconds before midnight the men stop, and everyone listens to the church bells ringing in the New Year. When the bells fall silent, the men resume beating with even greater vigor. Fifteen minutes or so of this racket is felt to be sufficient to drive away the evil spirits for the rest of the year.

Chlaüsefieber, or Chlaus fever, strikes the small village of Urnäsch in the canton of Appenzell on New Year's Day. The cherished tradition of Silvesterkläuse finds even the youngest Swiss dressed and ready for the celebration.

## The Silvesterkläuse of Urnäsch

Perhaps the most elaborate New Year's procession of all takes place in the small community of Urnäsch in the canton of Appenzell. In certain households there, Christmas may come and go without much fanfare. Instead the festive days may find the man of the house tromping through the woods collecting moss and greenery, or hunched over a large plywood and cardboard object, painstakingly sewing on thousands of small glass pearls. This man—and many like him—is overcome by *Chläuse-fieber*, or Chlaus fever, the mixture of excitement and performance jitters that grips participants in the annual New Year's custom of the *Silvesterkläuse*, or *Chläuse* for short.

The Silvesterkläuse is a cherished tradition in Urnäsch

Dressed in the traditional garb of Chläuse, participants greet family and friends after a performance of bell ringing and singing *(above)*. The Schö-Wüeschti, or less-ugly Chläuse *(right)*, cover themselves with a variety of natural materials arranged for a decorative effect.

A Schöne, or pretty, Chläuse poses for a moment along his route to show off his costume. The cowbells he shoulders can weigh as much as 30 pounds each *(right)*. Other pretty Chläuse dress as womenfolk complete with rosy-cheeked masks and towering headdresses *(below)*.

and a handful of other Appenzell villages, including Herisau, Schwellbrunn, Hundwil, Stein, Schönengrund, and Waldstatt. However, the men of Urnäsch proudly consider their performance of the custom the purest and most artful. In the Chläuse, groups of men dressed in ornate costumes and carrying enormous bells parade through the town and countryside on the modern New Year's Eve, December 31, and on January 12, the old New Year's Eve according to the Julian calendar. The men stop at the homes of their friends, town notables, and others who appreciate the Chläuse, where they put on a performance of rhythmic bell ringing and *Zäuerli*, the yodeling that is typical of that region. Although children and adolescent boys also take part, women do not: Chläuse is strictly for men.

Early on the morning of New Year's Eve, the participants begin the preparations for their long day. First they put on their costumes. There are three types of Chläuse. The costumes of the *Schöne*, or pretty, Chläuse are the most ornate. Some pretty Chläuse dress as menfolk, with velvet jackets and britches, white stockings, and clean hiking boots. Their faces are covered by a pink-faced mask, and a black pipe known as *Lendauerli* hangs from its lips. The menfolk carry two enormous cowbells weighing as much as 30 pounds each, one at the front, one at the back, slung over their shoulders with leather straps.

Other Chläuse do their best to earn their title of "pretty" by dressing as womenfolk. A velvet skirt covered by a white apron, a velvet vest over a puffy white blouse bedecked with red bows, long white gloves, and white stockings make up the ensemble. The accompanying mask is a smiling, rosy-cheeked doll face with a flower painted at the corner of the mouth. The men dressed as womenfolk carry a rack of 13 round bells, called a *Rolleträger*, similar to harness bells.

Perhaps the most spectacular item of the pretty Chläuse costumes is the headdress. It is 4 to 5 feet wide and towers 2 to 3 feet high. The outside is decorated with foil, mirrors, and thousands of glass beads. On the headdress is a scene depicting some important aspect of everyday life in the area. These headdresses are often true works of art, representing two or three years of planning and hundreds of hours of work.

On the other end of the spectrum are the *Wüeschti*, or ugly Chläuse. These men cover old clothes with natural materials such as snail shells, bark, leaves, moss, pine and juniper branches, pine cones, and nuts. Some cover their faces with vegetation. But others sculpt frightening papier-mâché demon masks complete with sharp teeth and red eyes.

The *Schö-Wüeschti*, or less-ugly Chläuse, are a relatively recent phenomenon. While the less-uglies use natural materials as do the uglies, they arrange them for a decorative effect. The first less-ugly Chläuse groups appeared in the 1960's.

Thus costumed, the Chläuse set out. When they reach a home at which they want to perform, they begin to ring their bells. The ringing is a musical endeavor, with particular rhythms and patterns that the most serious Chläuse groups rehearse diligently to perfect. Then the bells are gradually silenced, and the Chläuse sing one or more Zäuerli. This singing is also a skill. And Appenzellers, appreciating fine singers, offer the Chläuse warm drinks, which they sip through their masks with a bent straw. As the Chläuse depart, they often receive a few francs.

Although participants and aficionados are fond of describing the Silvesterkläuse as an ancient fertility rite, no one knows the actual origins of the custom. It is known that it goes back at least to the 1600's, when church officials criticized the superstitious custom of "walking around at night with bells and making noise." Documents from the 1700's indicate that the Chläuse did not have many fans among the government officials, either. The state council issued a decree in 1744 stating that the "obscene and aggravating disguisement on the occasion of the so-called Klausen at Christmas and New Year will be forbidden and punished." This antipathy persisted into the 1900's. It was only after the 1920's that the public began to appreciate the custom.

## Berthold's Day

January 2 brings the celebration of *Bertholdstag*, or Berthold's Day, in some parts of Switzerland. In certain regions, this day was traditionally celebrated as a nut

Residents of Hallwil celebrate the Bärzelitag on January 2. Dressed in costume, participants wreak havoc on their own village and then share the joy with neighboring communities. The mischief ends with a meal shared by all.

festival. Children began collecting nuts in late autumn, and when Berthold's Day came, they played nut games, feasted on nut goodies, sang, and performed folk dances. In other areas, neighborhood processions, meals in local pubs, and general merriment were the order of the day.

In Hallwil, January 2 is the *Bärzelitag*, and the celebration has elements of a pagan spring-renewal ritual. Fifteen young, unmarried adults dress in costumes and masks—five as the "green," five as the "parched brown," and the remaining five as a camel and its drivers. During the day, the costumed groups run through the village, pulling pranks. When they have exhausted all opportunities for mischief in their own village, they make similar runs in neighboring towns. The day ends with a meal shared by all.

## Epiphany

Epiphany is an important celebration in Catholic Switzerland. But even this holy day has a pagan connection. In ancient times, the 12 *Rauchnächte* (literally, "smoke nights"), which were nights when the spirits supposedly rose and wandered the earth, ended on January 6. Households and churches celebrate Epiphany by adding the final element to their nativity scenes—figures of the Three Wise Men. In many cities, towns, and villages today, men dressed as the Wise Men collect money for charity on that day. Recently, modern-day Wise Men in Basel collected more than $35,000, to benefit a children's hospital.

On Epiphany, many families bake a special sweet bread called *Gâteau des Rois* (kings' cake) in French and

The Wise Men, traveling by camel, make their appearance on Epiphany, January 6, in many villages, towns, and cities of Switzerland. Along their way they often collect money for charity.

Bakers in the town of Appenzell display a huge Gâteau des Rois (king's cake), the traditional sweet bread for the Epiphany. Made of individual balls of dough stuck together before baking, there is no doubt that this treat is fit for a king.

*Dreikönigskuche* (three-kings' cake) in Swiss-German. This loaf is made by sticking together lumps of dough before baking so that it comes hot from the oven as a ring of easy-to-separate rolls. Inside one of the rolls is a little token—a plastic crown, king, Madonna, or other figure. The lucky diner who receives the roll with the token has the privilege of wearing a crown and is promised good luck for the whole year.

In Ticino, some families celebrate the Epiphany the Italian way, with a visit from Befana. According to legend, Befana was an old lady—some accounts say a witch—whom the Three Wise Men approached for directions to Bethlehem. But Befana was so engrossed in her household chores that she could not put her broom down for even a moment to help them. No sooner had they gone on their way, though, than poor Befana began to feel ashamed that she had not helped them. She set out after them but never caught up with them. To this day, she roams the world at Epiphany giving gifts to well-behaved children and punishing the naughty ones with whacks from her broom. In some households, the children anticipate Befana's visit by hanging a *stivale,* or boot, by the fireplace. Befana comes down the chimney and fills the stivale with presents.

## So ends the season

While Epiphany is the official end of the Christmas season in Switzerland, perhaps it is fitting to mention one final holy day: the *Festa di San Antonio,* the Feast of Saint Anthony, which celebrates the humble beasts of the earth. On January 17, in the canton of Ticino, farmers bring their animals to church for a blessing. From the donkeys and horses ridden by St. Nicholas and pulling his sleigh; to the barnyard animals who supposedly talk on Christmas Eve; to the ox, lamb, and cow that paid the first respects to the newborn baby Jesus, animals have their part in the Christmas celebration. Perhaps the Feast of St. Anthony can be interpreted as a way to make sure their contributions—at Christmas and throughout the year—are not overlooked.

# Kissing Dove Garland

*These doves make a decorative garland
to hang on your tree or wall.*

## What to Do

**1** Use tracing paper and pencil to copy the dove pattern below. Cut out the pattern you have traced.

**2** Accordion-pleat the white paper in 4½-inch lengths.

**3** Tape the cut-out pattern onto the pleated paper so that the beak and tail touch the folds.

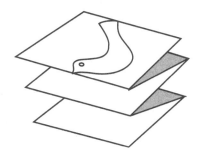

**4** Keep the pattern taped to the pleated paper. Tape the paper to a foam pad or sheet of corrugated cardboard to protect your work surface. Use a pushpin to poke holes through all layers of the pleated paper, following the design on the pattern.

**5** Cut out the doves following the pattern, making sure that they remain connected at the tail and beak.

**6** Carefully unfold the paper and you will have a dove garland. To make a longer garland, tape several of these together end-to-end.

## Materials

- tracing paper
- pencil
- pointed scissors
- lightweight white paper (watercolor, construction or other papers from the art or crafts store)
- masking tape
- foam pad or sheet of corrugated cardboard
- pushpin

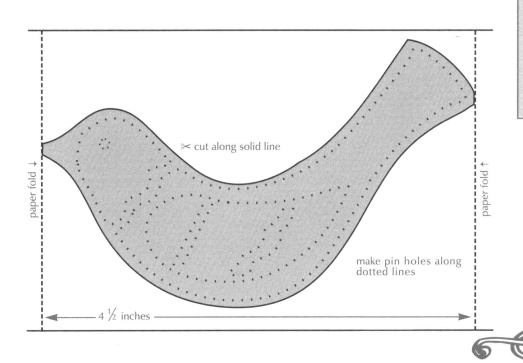

paper fold →

paper fold ↑

✄ cut along solid line

make pin holes along dotted lines

← 4 ½ inches →

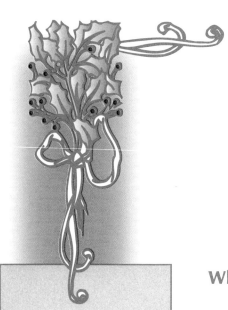

# Natural Bell Ornament

*Make a tree decoration inspired by the Silvesterkläuse's Schö-Wüeschti.*

## Materials

- tracing paper
- pencil
- cardboard
- scissors
- red or white satin ribbon, about 6 inches long
- 2 jingle bells
- craft glue
- newspaper
- moss (found in a craft or floral shop)
- an assortment of seeds such as pumpkin, sunflower, squash
- tweezers (optional)

## What to Do

**1** Trace this bell pattern onto tracing paper with a pencil. Cut out the pattern and draw the bell onto the cardboard. Cut out the cardboard bell shape.

**2** Thread the ribbon through the jingle bells' metal loops. Then, make a loop with the ribbon and place the ends on each side of the bell shape and secure with a dab of glue. Allow the glue to dry, following the instructions on the glue bottle.

**3** Cover your work surface with newspaper. Spread glue thoroughly on one side of the bell shape and cover it with half of the moss. After the glue has dried, gently turn the bell shape over and repeat the process.

**4** On one side of the bell shape, glue half of the seeds on top of the moss. You can create your own pattern or use the pattern below as a sample. Don't worry about getting glue on the sides of the seeds—it will

be clear when it dries. A pair of tweezers may help you position the seeds.

**5** Gently turn the bell shape over and repeat step 4 on the other side.

**6** Experiment with different kinds of seeds to make different designs. The larger the seed, the easier it will be to glue. You will find a selection at garden stores and health-food stores. Try melon, pumpkin, sesame, squash, and poppy seeds, as well as hulled oats.

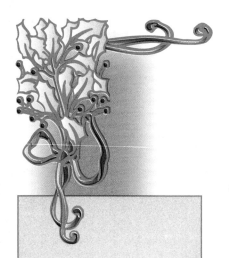

# Chocolate Advent Tree

*Eat a yummy chocolate every day and count down to the arrival of your favorite bearded fellow dressed in red!*

## Materials

- one or more bare twiggy branches about 24 inches long
- large, deep container such as a flower pot (at least 6 inches in diameter*)
- pebbles to fill the container
- thin ribbon, about 8 feet
- transparent tape
- 24 foil-wrapped chocolates
- 24 self-adhesive labels
- felt-tipped pen
- kissing dove garland (see page 65)
- natural bell ornament (see page 66)
- assorted ribbons to make bows for decoration
- wide red ribbon
- pine cones, pine sprigs, holly sprigs

*the larger the branches, the larger and deeper the pot should be

## What to Do

**1** Place the branch or branches in the center of the container, making sure that the bottom of each branch touches the bottom of the container.

**2** While holding the branches straight, pour the pebbles into the container. Fill the container to the top with pebbles so that each branch is held securely.

**3** Cut the thin ribbon into 4-inch lengths. Tape the ends of each piece to the back of a foil-wrapped chocolate, creating a loop from which to hang the chocolate.

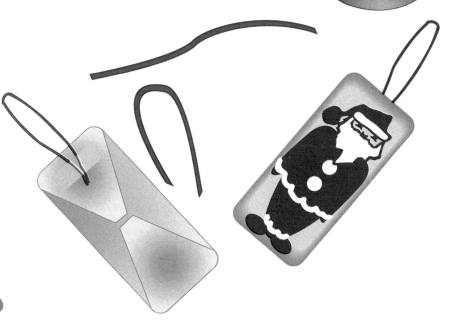

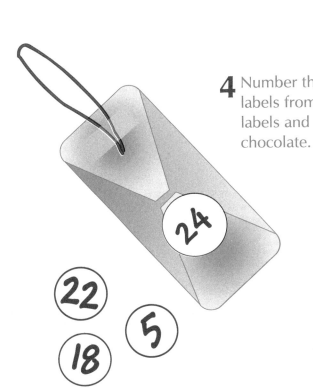

**4** Number the self-adhesive labels from 1 to 24. Peel off the labels and put one on each chocolate.

**5** Hang the chocolates on the tree branch. The chocolates should not be hung in numerical order.

**6** You can further decorate the tree branch with the dove garland, the bell ornament, and ribbon bows.

**7** To decorate the container, use the wide red ribbon to make a bow, then wrap it around the container.

**8** Place pine cones and pine and holly sprigs around the base of the tree branch to cover the pebbles.

**9** To count down to Christmas, start on December 1. Each day, search for the numbered chocolate that corresponds to the date. Yum!

# Swiss Chalet Wrap

*This sack is handy for wrapping a present that is oddly shaped or too big for a box.*

## Materials

- brown paper bag large enough to hold the present you want to wrap

- ruler

- pencil

- scissors

- white glue

- 2 sheets of dark-colored construction paper, slightly larger than your brown paper bag*

- construction paper of various colors

*if necessary, tape several sheets of paper together to get large-enough sheets

## What to Do

**1** Place the present you wish to wrap inside a brown paper bag. Fold down the top of the bag.

**2** Trim a sheet of dark-colored construction paper so that it is a slightly wider rectangle than the width of the brown bag. Trim the height of the construction paper to be about ⅓ the height of the brown bag. Fold the trimmed construction paper in half to match the illustration at right. On the folded paper, draw a diagonal line from the top left corner to the bottom right corner. Cut along this diagonal line. Unfold the paper. You should have a triangular shape. Repeat this process so that you have two triangles.

paper fold →

✂ cut along diagonal line

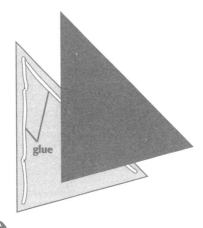

glue

**3** On one of the triangles, draw a line of glue on the two long sides as shown. Then glue the other triangle to it. This will become the roof.

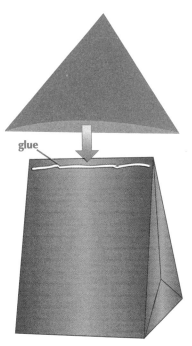

**4** Draw a line of glue on each side of the top of the paper bag. Place the open end of the two glued triangles over the top of the paper bag to glue the triangles to the bag. Allow the glue to dry, following the directions on the bottle.

**5** Cut thin strips out of colored construction paper. Glue them onto the triangular roof shape as well as on the bag to create the distinctive crisscross pattern found on some Swiss chalets (see illustration at right). Also cut out rectangular and square shapes for windows, shutters, and a door.

**6** Glue all of the shapes to the front and back of the paper bag so that it looks like the one shown here.

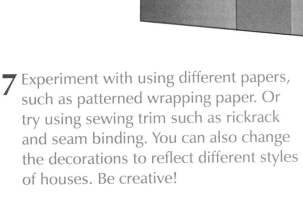

**7** Experiment with using different papers, such as patterned wrapping paper. Or try using sewing trim such as rickrack and seam binding. You can also change the decorations to reflect different styles of houses. Be creative!

# Swiss Recipes

### Capretto (Roasted Kid)

2 tbsp. butter
1 tsp. ground sage
1 tbsp. fresh mint
¼ tsp. cinnamon
⅛ tsp. nutmeg

2 lbs. boneless kid (young goat),
   cut into bite-sized pieces
salt and pepper to taste
1 cup sherry
1 cup cream
1 tbsp. rum

Melt the butter in a Dutch oven over medium heat. Add the
sage, mint, cinnamon, and nutmeg and stir for 3 minutes.
Sprinkle the meat with salt and pepper to taste and toss to coat.
Add the meat to the butter mixture and brown on all sides.
Lower the heat and add the sherry. Simmer, covered, until the
meat is tender. Remove the meat and keep warm. Add the
cream and rum to the Dutch oven; stir well. Bring mixture to
a boil and continue to boil until mixture is reduced by a third.
Serve the meat on a bed of rice and top with sauce. Makes
4 to 6 servings.

### Risotto

½ cup butter
1 small onion, finely chopped
1 cup rice
1 cup beef stock

1 cup dry white wine
salt and pepper to taste
¼ cup grated
   Parmesan cheese

Melt butter in a heavy saucepan over medium heat. Add the
onion and sauté until transparent. Add the rice; cook over
medium heat, stirring constantly, 2 minutes, or until the rice is
translucent. Add the beef stock, wine, and salt and pepper; cover
and simmer over low heat 20 minutes or until rice is tender and
liquid is absorbed. Top with cheese. Makes 6 servings.

## Rösti (Swiss Potatoes)

4 large baking potatoes
1 small onion
3 tbsp. butter

3 tbsp. vegetable oil
salt and pepper to taste

Skin and grate potatoes and onion; set aside. Heat butter and oil in a large skillet. Spread potatoes and onions in the pan and press down slightly with a spatula; cover. Cook over medium-low heat until the bottom of the potatoes and onions is golden brown. Turn mixture over and brown the other side. Season with salt and pepper to taste. Makes 6 servings.

## Onion Tart

**Dough**
2 cups presifted all-purpose flour
¼ tsp. salt
½ cup shortening
4 tbsp. ice water

**Filling**
2 tbsp. butter
10 medium onions, thinly sliced
salt and pepper to taste
1 cup milk
1 cup cream
3 tbsp. flour
2 eggs, well beaten
1 cup Swiss cheese, shredded

To make the dough, combine the flour and salt. Cut in the shortening until particles the size of small peas form. Add water. Stir to form a stiff dough. Knead dough on a lightly floured surface. Roll out to fit a buttered pie pan. Prick dough with a fork. Set aside.

To make the filling, melt the butter in a large skillet; add the onions and salt and pepper to taste. Sauté the onions until golden brown. In a medium bowl combine the milk and cream. Gradually add the flour; blend until smooth. Beat in the eggs and cheese. Add the sautéed onions.

Pour the filling into the dough-lined pan. Bake in a preheated 350° oven 30 minutes. Raise oven temperature to 400° and bake 5 minutes longer or until the top is browned. Serve immediately. Makes 6 servings.

## Änisbrötli (Anise Cookies)

3 eggs
1½ cups sugar
2 tbsp. aniseed
rind of one lemon

2 cups all-purpose flour
1 tsp. baking powder

Beat the eggs until light. Gradually add sugar, beating well after each addition. Continue to beat mixture for 15 minutes. Stir in aniseed and lemon rind. In a separate bowl, sift the flour with the baking powder. Gradually add flour mixture to form a stiff dough. Knead dough on a lightly floured surface, then cut into four equal pieces. Roll each piece into strips, 1 inch thick. Cut strips into 3-inch lengths. Nick each strip 3 times to the depth of ½ inch. Shape strips into U's, keeping the nicked edge outside. Place the cookies on greased cookie sheets. Allow to stand overnight at room temperature. Bake in a preheated 300° oven 15 minutes. Makes 2 dozen cookies.

## Mailänderli (Christmas Butter Cookies)

1 cup unsalted butter, softened
½ cup sugar
grated rind of 1 lemon
juice of 1 lemon

3 eggs
2½ cups presifted all-purpose
  flour
1 egg yolk, well beaten

In a large bowl, cream butter and sugar until light and fluffy. Add lemon rind and lemon juice. Beat in eggs, one at a time, mixing well after each addition. Gradually stir in flour. Knead the dough until it is smooth and not sticky. If it is too sticky, add small amounts of flour until it clears the fingers. Wrap the dough in plastic wrap and chill overnight.

Roll out the dough between two pieces of waxed paper to a ¼-inch thickness. Cut the dough with small cookie cutters. Place cookies on greased, floured cookie sheets. Brush with beaten egg yolk. Bake in a preheated 350° oven about 12 to 15 minutes, or until golden. Store cookies in an airtight container. Makes 4 dozen cookies.

## Basler Brunsli (Chocolate~Almond Cookies)

2 cups ground almonds, divided
1¼ cups granulated sugar
1 cup grated semi-sweet chocolate
1 tsp. cinnamon
½ tsp. ground cloves
2 egg whites, lightly beaten

Combine 1½ cups almonds with sugar, chocolate, cinnamon, and cloves in a large mixing bowl. Add egg whites. Knead the mixture to form a stiff dough. If the mixture is too sticky, add more almonds as necessary. If the mixture crumbles, add water, 1 teaspoon at a time, until the consistency is right.

On a surface lightly coated with granulated sugar, press the dough to ¼-inch thickness. Cut out cookies with a heart-shaped cookie cutter dipped in granulated sugar; place on cookie sheets lined with greased aluminum foil. Allow cookies to stand at room temperature for about 2 hours. Bake cookies in preheated 300° oven 15 minutes. Cool on wire racks; store in an airtight container. Makes 2 to 3 dozen cookies.

## Muesli

3 tbsp. quick-cooking oatmeal
3 tbsp. water
1 tbsp. fresh lemon juice
1 tbsp. honey
1 large apple
1 tbsp. slivered almonds

Make the oatmeal according to the package directions, using 3 tablespoons of oatmeal and water; add more water or oats to get the consistency you prefer.  Stir in the lemon juice and honey. Grate the apple, skin and all, into the muesli. Stir in almonds. Feel free to use any fresh fruit to replace the apple. Makes 1 serving.

## Züpfe (Braided Bread)

1 package active dry yeast
¼ cup lukewarm water
¾ cup lukewarm milk
1 tbsp. sugar

1 tsp. salt
1 egg
3 cups all-purpose flour
1 egg yolk, slightly beaten

Dissolve the yeast in the lukewarm water; set aside. Combine the milk, sugar, salt, and egg in a large bowl; mix well. Stir in dissolved yeast. Gradually add the flour until a soft dough forms. Turn the dough out on a floured surface and knead until smooth and elastic, about 5 minutes. Place the dough in a greased bowl; cover and allow to rise until doubled in bulk, about 2 hours. Punch down the dough and divide into 2 equal pieces. On a lightly floured surface, shape each piece into a 14-inch rope. Twist the pieces together, crossing one over the other and pinching at the ends. Place the bread on a greased cookie sheet, cover, and allow to rise another hour. Brush bread with egg yolk. Bake in a preheated 425° oven 20 to 25 minutes or until golden. Makes 1 loaf.

## Dough for Spicy Pear Roll (see recipe card)

2 packages active dry yeast
½ tsp. sugar
½ cup lukewarm water
¼ cup unsalted butter
¾ cup milk

½ cup sugar
1 tsp. salt
1 egg, well beaten
5 cups bread flour

Dissolve yeast and ½ teaspoon sugar in the lukewarm water; set aside. Heat together butter and milk until the butter melts; pour into a large bowl and add sugar, salt, and egg. Allow mixture to cool. Stir in dissolved yeast. Add enough flour to form a soft dough. Knead dough on a lightly floured surface. Return dough to bowl; cover and allow to rise in a warm place until doubled in size, about 1 hour.

# Swiss Carols

## Tedlei, O Fideivels
## (O Come, All Ye Faithful)

J.F. Wade

Andante moderato

1. Ted - lei, o fi - dei - vels,
2. Bein spert cun pre - mu - ra
3. Na - dal, o fi - dei - vels,

la le - grei - vla no - va: na - schius ei il
da lur mun - ta ne - ras ar - ri - van tiel
tgei le - grei - vla fia - sta! Ve - gni tuts, vo -

Se - gner a Bet - le - - hem.
Se - gner ils buns pa - sturs.
gni cun grond le - gher - ment!

Leu sur la stal - la con - tan - mel - li
O tgei le - gri - a, igl af - fon els
Il car Sal - va - der nus tuts be - ne -

aun - ghels: Ve - ni te, a - do - re - mus, ve - ni - te, a - do -
an - flan:
de - scha:

re - mus, ve - ni - te, a - do - re - - mus Do - mi - num.

# The Star of Bethlehem Shines Bright

Music and Text by Paul Burkhard

Andante

1. The star of Beth - le - hem shines bright, fol - low it now this ho - ly night. Tru - ly it
2. The star leads to the Babe who sleeps, while Vir - gin Mar - y vig - il keeps. Our Lord is
3. Sing praise, re - joice for this new star, fol - low the road though it be far. His birth will

is a love - - - ly star.
still so weak and small,
bring an end of strife,

Come, ev - 'ry - one, from near and far.
but He will soon rule o'er us all,
and give to us e - ter - nal life,

come, ev - 'ry - one, from near and far.
but He will soon rule o'er us all.
and give to us e - ter - nal life.

# Acknowledgments

| | | | |
|---|---|---|---|
| Cover | Mon-Tresor from Panoramic Images, Ltd.; Blume, Bildagentur Baumann AG | 36 | M. Baumann, Bildagentur Baumann AG |
| 2 | Peter Studer, Bildagentur Baumann AG | 37 | Perret, Bildagentur Baumann AG |
| 6 | Swiss National Tourist Office | 38 | Emanuel Ammon, AURA |
| 9 | M. Baumann, Bildagentur Baumann AG; Perret, Bildagentur Baumann AG | 39 | Comet Photo AG |
| | | 40-41 | Swiss National Tourist Office |
| 12 | D. Manzardo, Bildagentur Baumann AG | 42 | Johann Wanner |
| | | 44 | Joann Seastrom* |
| 14 | Gensetter, Bildagentur Baumann AG | 45 | Ringier; Joann Seastrom*; Joann Seastrom* |
| 16 | Sharkie, Bildagentur Baumann AG; H. Reusser, Keystone Press AG | 46 | Comet Photo AG; Dale Debolt* |
| | | 47 | Comet Photo AG |
| 17 | Keystone Press AG | 48 | Joe Viesti, Viesti Associates, Inc. |
| 18 | PRISMA from Viesti Associates, Inc. | 51 | Dale DeBolt* |
| | | 52 | PRISMA from Viesti Associates, Inc. |
| 20 | Comet Photo AG; M. Baumann, Bildagentur Baumann AG | 53 | Viesti Associates, Inc. |
| | | 54-55 | PRISMA from Viesti Associates, Inc. |
| 21 | PRISMA from Viesti Associates, Inc. | 56 | Viesti Associates, Inc. |
| 23 | Nestle | 57 | Lanz, Ringier; PRISMA, Van-Hoorick from Viesti Associates, Inc. |
| 25 | Brännhage, PRISMA from Viesti Associates, Inc. | | |
| 26 | Davis, PRISMA from Viesti Associates, Inc. | 58 | Swiss National Tourist Office |
| | | 61 | Comet Photo AG |
| 27 | Emanuel Ammon, AURA | 62-63 | Snozzi, Ringier |
| 28 | Dale DeBolt* | 64 | Dale DeBolt* |
| 29 | Dale DeBolt*; PRISMA from Viesti Associates, Inc. | | |
| 30 | Brännhage, PRISMA from Viesti Associates, Inc. | | |
| 33 | C.O. Roth, Bildagentur Baumann AG; Emanuel Ammon, AURA | | |
| 34 | Comet Photo AG; Emanuel Ammon, AURA | | |

Ribbon borders, map, and craft illustrations:
    Sarah Figlio*
Marzipan:
    Bonny M. Davidson, Faerie Castle Marzipan*
Advent Calendar:
    Gwen Connelly*
Recipe cards:
    World Book photos by Dale DeBolt*
Music:
    Jonathan Norton*

All entries marked with an asterisk (*) denote illustrations created exclusively for World Book, Inc.